To Lynne

Sir John Soane's Museum, London

Text
Stefan Buzas

Photographs
Richard Bryant

Wasmuth

Editor: Axel Menges

© 1994 Ernst Wasmuth Verlag, Tübingen/Berlin
Third, revised edition 1999
ISBN 3-8030-2714-4

Design: Axel Menges

Printed in Korea.

Contents

»Architecture is an Art purely of Invention« – The house of John Soane

»There must be an Order and just Proportion, Intricacy with Simplicity in the Component parts, Variety in the Mass, and Light and Shadow in the whole, so as to produce the varied sensations of gaiety and melancholy, of wildness and even of surprise and wonder …«

»Architecture is an Art purely of invention, and invention is the most painful and the most difficult of the human mind.«

John Soane, *Lectures on Architecture*

John Soan – the »e« came later – was the son of a small builder in Goring, Berkshire, and little is known of his childhood. John and Mary Soan had seven children and the last, the future architect, was born on 10 September 1753. As a boy he worked for his elder brother William who was a bricklayer, but soon he felt the urge to »better himself« and before long he obtained an introduction to the Clerk of the Works to the City of London, none other than George Dance.

It may be highly relevant that, after Soane was taken into Dance's office, his master was commissioned to design the new prison at Newgate. This monumental project, perhaps Dance's masterpiece, must have already impressed upon the young student the fundamental strength of the classical language and from Dance he also learnt the need for accurate and carefully rendered drawings. By 1771, at the age of 18, after working also in Henry Holland's office, he felt sufficiently confident to apply to the Royal Academy School. It is not known what he submitted as testimony of his abilities and skill, but it was competent enough for him to be entered into the register of students. Five years on, the enthusiastic and committed student was rewarded by receiving the Academy's Gold Medal for a Triumphal Bridge design as was of-ficially confirmed by the President Sir Joshua Reynolds. An account quotes the great painter as having presented the medal to the youngster with this prophetic eulogy: »… He bestowed on Mr Soan /this prize/ with such appropriate remarks upon his genius, such commendation of his performance, and such prophetic hopes of his perseverance, and consequent success, as were … far more valuable than even the medal itself.«[1]

After much study of classical architecture, especially through the many etchings of Piranesi who remained his life-long inspiration, he was sufficiently mature and ready to apply for a travelling scholarship. A diary entry by Joseph Farington relates that »… Soane told me that before he applied to the Academy, he waited on Sir Wm. Chambers, whom he prevailed upon to show some drawings to the King, which Sir William told Soane his Majesty approved, and directed that he shd. be sent to Rome by the Academy …«[2] After some delay Soane was sent a letter at the end of 1777 confirming his election to the King's travelling studentship together with an allowance and travelling expenses that enabled him to start on his Grand Tour in March 1778. Although his journeys took him as far as Sicily, in Rome he had the rare fortune of being introduced to the great Piranesi. The old man, nearing death, made a gift to the admiring young man of four of his engravings from the »Vedute di Roma« series, and these – the Pantheon, the Arches of Constantine and Septimus Severus and the tomb of Cecilia Metella – were perhaps his most treasured possessions and also perhaps indications of his tendency towards a dual influence that made the art historian Henry-Russell Hitchcock define him as a »romantic classicist«. These engravings hang to this day in his house in Lincoln's Inn Fields in London.

But before recording the events leading up to the design of his famous house, an account of a meeting in Rome has to be told as it was the first step towards

1. John Soane, Triumphal Bridge, 1776. Joseph Michael Gandy, 1799 (?). (SJSM = Sir John Soane's Museum, Drawer 12/5/7)
2. Nathaniel Dance, John Soane at the age of twenty-one, 1774. (SJSM, P 317)

establishing Soane's career in England. The amiable and conscientious young man, having sought the company of eminent travellers, was introduced to Frederick Hervey, Bishop of Derry. This patron of the arts took to the young architect instantly, and soon he was in frequent attendance. Amongst the gifts from the cultured cleric Soane received a lavishly bound volume of Palladio's *Quattro Libri* and other classical records. Having decided to travel to Naples the Bishop invited Soane to accompany him; but soon after Hervey left Italy having been informed of his brother's death upon which he inherited the title of the 4th Earl of Bristol. Letters from the Earl-Bishop suggesting employment as his architect ended Soane's travels and experiences in the land of inexhaustible architectural wonders, and the end of June 1780 saw him back in England. Whilst the Earl's plans for work at his seat at Ickworth in Suffolk came to nothing it gave him the impetus to establish his own practice in London from which all subsequent great projects stemmed.

His prospering practice, with several important commissions, encouraged Soane to contemplate marriage. During his previous work on Dance's Newgate Gaol he made the acquaintance of the City Surveyor George Wyatt. Wyatt lived in Albion Place with his favourite niece Elizabeth Smith, and soon the architect noted in his diary visits to and outings with the 23-year-old attractive girl. The register in a Lambeth church records the marriage of »John Soan of the Parish of St Marylebone to Elizabeth Smith of this Parish by special licence«, on 21 August 1784.[3]

Thanks to his wife gaining an inheritance and his appointment as architect to the Bank of England in 1788, Soane was able to consider the purchase of a house in the rural surroundings of Ealing, so appropriate as a showpiece for a young ambitious architect. The property he desired, Pitzhanger Manor, belonged

to the family of Thomas Gurnell, who was Dance's father-in-law, and a payment of £4,500 assured him the ownership. In 1800 the property was his.

He replaced the earlier part of the Manor, which had been enlarged by Dance in 1768, with a design which introduces us to the features that would later mature in his London house. With Pitzhanger we enter the realm of Soane's domestic architecture as well as his spiritual world. The façade is an echo of his Italian experiences and in fact a remarkable adaptation of the triumphal arches he saw and measured. Here he already demonstrated one of his great abilities of mastering scale. We shall meet this skill throughout this house as well as at his London residence. The scale is monumental, the dimensions are domestic – a rare achievement!

Pitzhanger was ready for occupation in 1804. The entrance, a narrow passage with steps up to the ground floor, shows his second skill, the use of the hidden light-source and its magical effect. The Breakfast Parlour and the Library are prototypes of what must be defined as his life-long preoccupation with mortality and, equally profoundly, with the collecting and display of objects which he believed enhanced the understanding of art and architecture as well as pointing to the dignity of man.

Soane had two sons. His belief that they would become the inheritors of his genius, in fact the dream of an architectural dynasty, was the source of his greatest and deepest disappointment. A trait of melancholia, combined with a conviction bordering on megalomania that his great abilities would be transmitted to his stock, indicates a character of unusual persistence. This dream, the »Pitzhanger dream«, as Dorothy Stroud called it, was soon to be shattered, and the house was sold in 1810. Neither son had shown any interest in it, and despite his elder son John's enforced study of architecture, it became clear that there was no spark that could be fanned into even a mild blaze. John's interest was for other matters, and a disapproved marriage alienated him from his father. His second son George meanwhile pursued a reluctant study in Cambridge and was, after coming down, taken in by a firm of solicitors to study law. He too was trapped into an unsuitable liaison and marriage, and an almost pathological hostility towards his father, revealed by an article he wrote in the *Champion* of 1815, was the final act of betrayal.

This short résumé sets the scene for Soane's all-pervading desire to establish a Pantheon of architectural inspiration in his London house, a desire that was to result in the creation of the »Poetry of Architecture«, a theme that is the heart and matter of this remarkable man.

Eight years before he acquired Pitzhanger, Soane had bought house No. 12 in Lincoln's Inn Fields. The site was, in his day, with its very large square, its lawns and trees, an almost rural surrounding. It was also conveniently placed for his frequent visits to the City, where the building of the Bank of England demanded his presence. No. 12 is a standard London terrace house in all essentials, but, after Soane had rebuilt it, it contained a room at the rear that presaged the Pitzhanger ideas and which was to be elaborated in the later adjoining house, No. 13, the subject of this monograph.

An interior perspective by Joseph Michael Gandy shows Soane seated at the round breakfast table examining a plan, while »Mrs Soane (is) presiding behind the tea kettle and the boys disporting themselves nearby«.[4] Here is an unmistakable Soanean room. The shallow attenuated, flattened cross vault, most daringly lopsided to centre it on the large window, gives a loftiness to a normal ceiling height, exaggerated by Gandy's disproportion of the furniture and figures. A table is seen by the window that indicates the architect's single-minded drive to work at all hours (his as-

sistants in the low office beyond the courtyard worked from 7 to 7 in the summer and 8 to 8 in the winter). The five rosettes on the underside of the arch above the fireplace are already indications of a motif that will be seen in the future Breakfast Parlour of No. 13, but with surprising results. On the wall, above the bookcases, hang the engravings Piranesi presented to him in Rome. The niches here and in the opposite wall house statuettes and »Etruscan« vases. The simulated trellis, a bower that recalled for him the shady terraces he must have sat under in Italy – a romantic desire in the often weak light of England – was to be conjured up in a different way later next door.

Before Pitzhanger occupied his mind Soane had a plan to enlarge his office, and he approached his neighbour with a proposal to acquire the stables behind No. 13. Mr Tyndale, the owner, agreed, with the stipulation that he remained in occupation of the house for a few years. Soane purchased the freehold of the property from him in 1808, and at first prepared designs for a Museum and a new office on the site of the stables at the back, which were built in 1808/09. No. 13 was somewhat wider and deeper than No. 12, and, when he reopened negotiations with Tyndale in 1810, they agreed that he would vacate the house provided he could take a lease on No. 12. When this was achieved, Soane demolished and rebuilt the front part of the house. Later, in 1823, he bought No. 14, which he also rebuilt, partly as an extension to his Museum and partly as offices which were leased. It must be realised that the creation of what is now his house and museum occupied Soane for almost 40 years. Not until 1834 did work finish, thus, three years before his death at the age of 84, the sumptuous conception became reality.

The T-shaped area, now at his disposal, consisting of the middle house and the rear plots of Nos.12 to 14 measures some 400 square metres. This group of three houses tempted Soane to consider an imposing

5. Extended façade for Nos. 13, 14 and 15 Lincoln's Inn Fields. Joseph Michael Gandy, 1813. (SJSM, Drawer 74/4/1)
6. Façade of No. 13 Lincoln's Inn Fields, 1812. Soane office. (SJSM, Drawer 14/6/2)

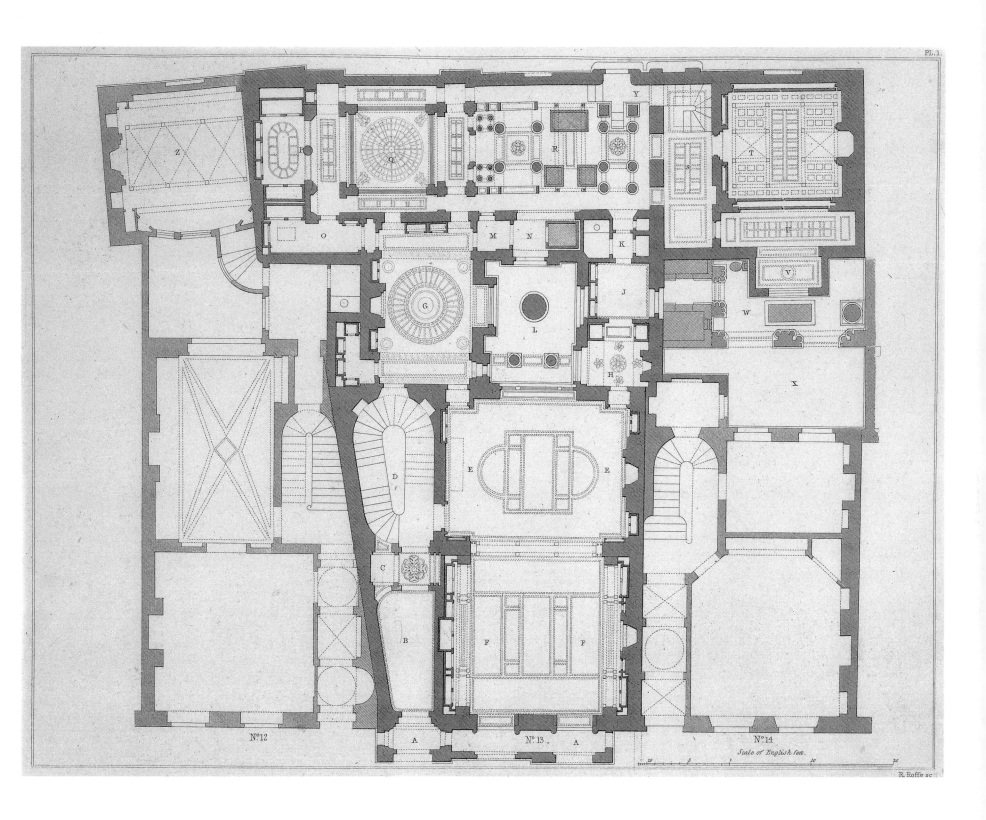

7. Ground-floor of Nos. 12, 13 and 14 Lincoln's Inn Fields. R. Roffe. (John Britton, *The Union of Architecture, Sculpture and Painting*, London, 1827, plate 1). Key: A Porch, B Outer Hall, C Inner Hall, D Staircase, E Dining-Room, F Library, G Breakfast Parlour, J Dressing-Room, H Study, K Dressing-Room Recess, L Monument Court (originally with the Pasticcio), M now Cupboard, N South Passage, O Ante-Room (enlarged in 1889 by James Wild), P Apollo Belvedere, Q Dome, R Colonnade, S Corridor, T Picture-Room, U Picture-Room Recess, V Nymph by Sir Richard Westmacott, W Monk's Tomb, X Monk's Yard, Y staircase to the Crypt, Z former Picture-Room, now site of the remodelled New Picture-Room.

composition of façades. Two drawings exist to show how he intended to rival the grand houses surrounding the Fields. The designs were in fact for Nos. 13, 14 and 15, suggesting that he may have considered owning even No. 15. Eventually he decided on Nos. 12 and 14 showing façades in the tradition of the typical Georgian house, with grey bricks and stone dressings. No. 13, however, showing his sharp individuality, was made of sterner stuff.

The underlying plan is still that of a London terrace house with railed area to the half-basement, steps up to the front door at the side, with two windows to the right and three windows to the two upper floors. A third floor was added in 1824, somewhat altering the proportion and the skyline. Out of this basic arrangement the appearance is unexpected. The ground and first floors project in front of the terrace and the centre bay of the second floor joins the smooth Portland stone face like a small aedicule, with balconies on both sides with female figures in the style of the Erechtheion caryatids. The six openings of ground and first floors carry semi-circular heads.

The »Loggia«, as Soane called this projection, was originally open, but was subsequently glazed in 1834. This, perhaps practical, alteration made for interesting internal spaces resulting in architectural surprises of great originality. On the façade are decorations, or rather incisions, that were to become a continuing theme in Soane's designs. These are linear substitutions for modelled decorations and characterize Soane's most personal feelings for attenuated and simplified motifs, an elegance that transcends his period into what we now perceive as »modern«. The inclusion of the open »loggia« into the interior spaces on the ground and first floors created narrow corridors, not much wider than one's shoulders. On the first floor this corridor became a volume of almost monumental scale. The detached slender columns, bundled like Roman fasces, in line with the piers between windows and linked to cross beams bearing busts, are tours-de-force of great daring. These, together with the many spatial surprises in the complex interiors, constitute the magic of Soane's mastery of scale and space.

Entering the house there is already a vista that presages rich experiences. The porphyry-coloured walls of the Entrance Hall, with various busts, torsos and roundels, lead into the Inner Hall that reveals the geometrical stair, with its widening curves dictated by the angled party-wall of No. 12. The Staircase walls are painted in imitation of giallo antico marble, a warm yellow that glows from the daylight of the roof lantern high above. The door ahead offers an inviting glimpse into the Breakfast Parlour, and the door to the right leads into the two principal rooms, the Dining-Room and Library.

Soane himself referred to these as »one room, separated only by two projecting piers«, a daring device that contains the desire for extending views into other spaces, a continuing principle that culminates in the multiple perspectives to come. The canopy that springs from these piers, spatially defining the two rooms, is of a remarkable outline. A drawing of 1825 shows this canopy as three semi-circular arches. This later changed into the tighter outline of the two outer arcs. These are now shortened just beyond the quarter circle and so allow a wider and shallower segment to connect them. Furthermore this almost Moresque motif is enriched by finials that in miniature represent,

8. Library and Dining-Room, No. 13 Lincoln's Inn Fields. H. Ansted, c. 1825. (SJSM, Vol. 82)
9. Monument Court, No. 13 Lincoln's Inn Fields. Edward Foxhall, c. 1813–18. (SJSM, Vol. 83,3)

10. Breakfast Parlour, No. 12 Lincoln's Inn Fields. Joseph Michael Gandy, 1798. (SJSM, Drawer 14/6/1)
11. Breakfast Parlour, No. 13 Lincoln's Inn Fields. Soane office, 2 November 1825. (SJSM, Vol. 82, 24)

be they in reversed form, Soane's all-pervading geometric theme – the hemisphere squared, or a dome with pendentives. The vertical surfaces of the canopy are further enriched by brackets shaped in the form of the springing of fan-vaults, an indication of his interest in gothic geometry. Similar canopies appear above the bookcases lining the two side walls of the front room, the Library. The mirrored surfaces behind the canopies introduce another remarkable feature of his interiors – the ubiquitous dissolution of space by means of reflections. This, it may be safe to say, is a characteristic invention, despite such illusory devices in the 18th century, for example at Versailles, or at the Sicilian Villa Palagonia.

The deep recesses of the full-length semi-circular-headed windows, facing the landscape of the square outside, increase the illusion of an interior extension, and here the fully mirrored centre pier creates a further surprise – the reflection of the large window in the Dining-Room opening onto the small courtyard beyond. Both the view into the trees outside and the reflected view of the enclosed space of the small court cannot fail to add to the contrast between the deep, warm feeling of comfort of the interior and the changing atmosphere of the world outside. At night sliding shutters, hidden during the day, are drawn across the windows. These, too, are fully mirrored and, with the mirror on the pier in the centre, present a reflective surface across the whole width of the room. Soane's one pleasure, after an intense day of work, was the enjoyment of the company of friends, and one can easily imagine the festive atmosphere of the room enhanced by the changing reflections of this nocturnal scene in the mirrors. Soane's constant desire to present his House and Museum in conditions that – subconsciously – recalled for him the sun-filled days in Italy revealed itself on the printed admission ticket to visitors. This warned them that there was »no admission in wet or dirty weather«. (Already by 1810 Soane had allowed visitors to view the museum part of his house.)

The Dining-Room, the first space off the stair hall, reveals other surprising devices. The convex circular mirrors, high up in the corners of the room, reflect almost disturbing views of adjoining spaces and objects and the mirrored strips that line the sash boxes and angled reveals of the large window dissolve any expected solids of vases and jars. Soane says that the »effect of these works is considerably heightened by the looking-glass in the splayed jambs of the windows«, an undoubted proof that his assemblages were most carefully calculated.

The small court beyond the large window is known as the Monument Court, named after a Pasticcio (pastiche), a column of a mixture of Romanesque, Soanean and even Hindu fragments that was put there in 1819 and removed in 1896, and is to be re-erected. A drawing by Edward Foxhall, a Soane pupil, shows this architectural fantasy as »an assemblage of ancient and modern Art«. This and most of the objects within and outside are all arrangements to show the universal value of architecture and point persistently to the duty of an architect who must, in Soane's words, think and feel as a poet, combine and embellish as a painter, and execute as a sculptor. This picturesque aesthetic continues to dominate space, vista and assembly throughout the house.

The Monument Court is flanked by three rooms on the east and west. On the east, what was a simple corridor linking the main rooms to the rear area soon became two inter-connecting rooms which here, as elsewhere, demonstrate that rare ability of transcending physical limitations. These rooms are almost of miniature size, but are in effect far larger in scale. The first closet is called the Study and contains a bewildering collection of objects: antique decorative fragments, cinerary urns, an ivory head of Inigo Jones and even a wax relief of a cadaver. With a window into the court the room is also lit by a lantern in the ceiling that, as elsewhere, is glazed with amber and yellow glass. A doorway leads into the next closet, the Dressing-Room. The ceiling is elaborately rich with a lantern as a piece of architecture in miniature, the centre being a model of the domical light in the new Hall of the Freemasons. Within the doorway beyond, a door to a cupboard contains an optical joke: a glazed light in that door is a brilliant game of mirror reflection as it is divided vertically by two mirrors at an angle of less than 180 degrees, thus refracting the image.

Two windows, facing east and west give onto the two courtyards, the Monument Court with the Pasticcio on one side and the suprising Monk's Yard, a totally different aspect of Soane's romantic inclination, on the other. Of the monk »Padre Giovanni« more later on, but this small light-well, at the rear of No. 14, is filled with sham ruins, and Soane's own description, so redolent of his fantasies, must be quoted in full to understand, if understanding were appropiate, how this lucid master of pure design can in another part of his personality pretend to live in a world of medieval ideals. He proceeds thus: »…The Ruins of a Monastery arrest the attention. The interest created in the mind of the spectator, on visiting the abode of the monk, will not be weakened by wandering among the ruins of his once noble monastery. The rich Canopy and other decorations of this venerable spot are objects which cannot fail to produce the most powerful sensations in the minds of the admirers of the piety of our forefathers, who raised such structures for the worship of the Almighty Disposer of events.«[5] A quotation at the end, taken from Horace, indicates that all this is not to be taken seriously. It is almost a relief to notice, in this world of the »gothick«, that the arches are surmounted by an 18th century Corinthian capital on which is a bust of George IV's brother, the Duke of York.

Reversing one's steps into the Dining-Room, a narrow door to the left of the large window opens into the celebrated Breakfast Parlour. This area is described as a dressing room on a plan of 1812, with appropriate water closet in the small space against the sloping party wall to No. 12, but later on that year a further plan already indicates the germ of the final configuration. A small freehand sketch of a section in the margin of the sheet reveals a domical outline in the centre with semi-circular tops to the narrow spaces on either sides. The plan, named a study, shows a dotted circle inscribed in a square centred on the window to the courtyard and a drawing of 1825, a plan and a section, documents in full detail the development of this early idea. Soane's *Description* of 1835 contains the following significant phrase: »… a succession of fanciful effects which constitute the Poetry of Architecture.« The fancy, or ornamental, is clearly evident again in the ef-

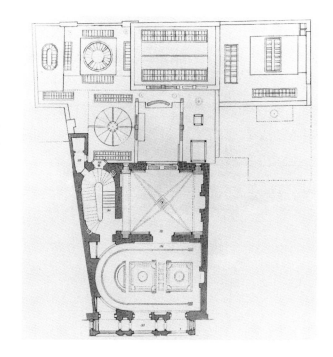

12. First-floor of No. 13 Lincoln's Inn Fields. (John Soane, *Description of the House and Museum*, London 1835, plate 33)
13. Loggia at the first floor of No. 13 Lincoln's Inn Fields. (John Soane, *Description of the House and Museum*, London 1835, plate 35)

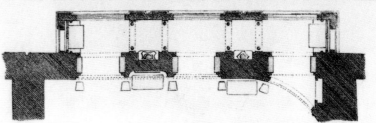

VIEW IN THE GALLERY OR RECESS, ADJOINING THE SOUTH DRAWING ROOM.

14. Rear part of Nos. 12, 13 and 14 Lincoln's Inn Fields.
Gladwin after C. J. Richardson. (John Britton, *The Union
of Architecture, Sculpture and Painting*, London, 1827,
plate 8)
15. Dome area, No. 13 Lincoln's Inn Fields. Soane office,
13 June 1808. (SJSM, PSA 34)

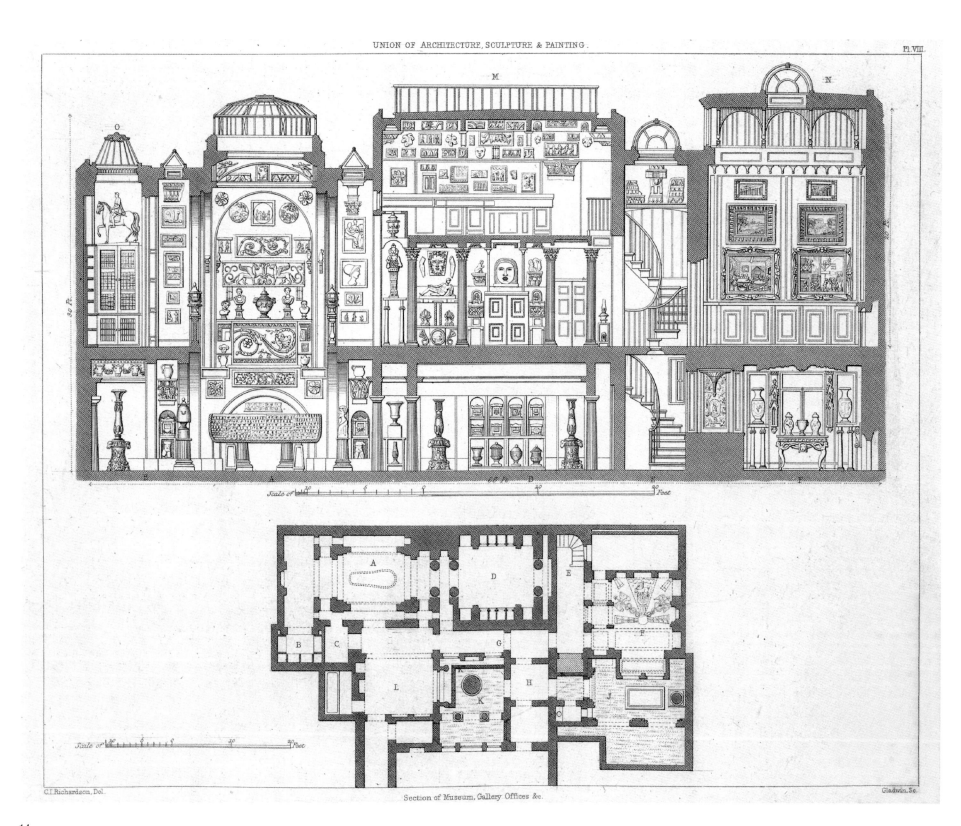

UNION OF ARCHITECTURE, SCULPTURE & PAINTING.

Pl. VIII.

Section of Museum, Gallery Offices &c.

C. J. Richardson, Del.

Gladwin, Sc.

fect of the numerous circular mirrors within »the rich canopy« of the spherical ceiling springing from four segmental arches.

Soane's constantly recurring theme of a domed ceiling is here of particular refinement. The grandiose views of its many variations in the Bank of England are here sensitively reduced to a proper scale, and the gently curving shallow dome flows almost weightlessly into the four pilasters. The sight of the monumental arches, cross-vaults and domes he saw in the ruins of the Roman Forum or those of Hadrian's villa near Tivoli is here tamed into the gentleness of his native land. Soane's spatial invention moves away and beyond the structural necessities of the Antique; the room is crowned by a seemingly weightless billowy sail, a sail-vault, where the curvature is continuous. The linear incisions, whilst echoing structure, are only used as a device to lead the eye towards the »oculus«, that circular opening in Roman structures that allowed light to stream in. A water-colour view of 1822 reveals painted angels in the corners of the dome (a repeat of the ceiling decoration in the Pitzhanger Breakfast Parlour). These were replaced by circular holes to let in daylight from the adjoining skylights and later were covered by convex mirrors that are now one of the many delights of this exquisite room. It is a proof of Soane's constant experimentation with the transmutation of spaces which was already noted as remarkable in his time. This also shows that his instincts were right to allow the concealed lighting of the two skylights to become fully effective: the light against the sharp edges of the two arches is the key to the illusion of a floating sail.

Soane's repeated feature of spherical ceilings must be considered of deep significance in his psyche. In several of Sir John Summerson's writings references are made to the »furniture of death« and to the architect's preoccupation with death. These dark thoughts are evident throughout the house, and one only needs to observe the vast collection of Roman funerary urns and grave ornaments to realize his feelings for the transience of life. One of the features of these objects that appealed to him most is the previously mentioned sectioned hemisphere, resulting in a dome and four pendentives. These »sail vaults« are the simplest of the geometric solutions of how to erect a dome over a square. It is not surprising, therefore, that the mausoleum he designed as the burial place of his wife, where he is also interred, is crowned by this simple, but strong geometry. Here the monolithic head-piece of the canopy is a much enlarged version of the lid of a cinerary urn, and Summerson relates this to the canopy in the Breakfast Parlour.[6]

Whatever one's thoughts and historical conclusions may be, this rich canopy is a joyous confirmation of the pleasures of life, and one can think of the morning's delights in that elegant room, in contrast to the deep tones of Pompeian red of the neighbouring Dining-Room and its lit candles on the laid table. Soane describes this central canopy as »springing from four segmental arches, supported by the same number of pilasters … The spandrels of the dome and the soffits of the arches are decorated with a number of mirrors. In the dome is an octangular lantern-light, enriched with eight Scriptural subjects in painted glass. At the north and south ends of the room are skylights, which diffuse strong light over the several Architectural and other works decorating the walls.« The mastery and

magic of light in this small room exemplifies the »poetry« he held so essential in his creations. One other remarkable detail must be mentioned: the pilasters are mirror faced. This device results in the illusion of weightlessness, as the strips of reflection confuse our perceptions and practically cause these supports to vanish. If proof be needed of Soane's subtlety of invention the Breakfast Parlour is a model of excellence, a jewel of a design.

Earlier a passing reference was made to certain similarities with Moresque architecture. Although such comparisons may be disputed it is interesting to read a passage in Arthur T. Bolton's book on the works of Soane (Bolton was the Curator of the Museum from 1917 to 1945). He writes »… One of the curiosities of Soane's interiors is the skill, worthy of an Arabian architect, with which he makes use of the reflective effect and brilliance of looking-glass, without overpassing the limit of that material, as a legitimate, if dangerous source of internal decorative effect.«[7] The certainty and serenity of such decorative effects are daring, but never dangerous.

In comparison with the ever changing vistas and rich surprises of the sequence of rooms on the ground floor, the first floor (or »One Pair Floor«) is a conventional plan derived from the standard arrangement of the London terrace house. Little surprises here, but nonetheless the two rooms are of unmistakable Soanean style. The South Drawing-Room's main features are its ceiling of two shallow barrel vaults within their squares and a segmental curved wall to the west, as well as the inclusion of the former outside loggia. The North Drawing-Room crowned by the typical shallow cross-vault, already seen in the Breakfast Parlour of No. 12, was originally furnished conventionally as it served as an »Anti-room« (sic) to the south facing Drawing-Room. Soane speaks of this ceiling as »partly groined and partly flat; a mode of decoration calculated to give variety and movement to the composition«.

This short description of the main domestic areas is only an outline. The innumerable objects, works of art, pictures, paintings, models and memorabilia can be appreciated only by a visit with the Museum's guide in hand. The variety and quantity is profuse, and it represents the wide interest of this obsessive collector. However there is, within all this profusion, one clearly stated intention of this restless man. In Soane's *Description* of 1835 his purpose is stated as »intended to benefit the artists of future generations, but is chiefly for the advancement of the architect«. This passionate aim conceals a much deeper meaning – his proud belief that his sons would take up their father's profession. This wishful, but unrealised, intention may well be the wellspring of his untiring search and acquisition of more and more works of art, in the hope that future generations would benefit from his passion for the Mother of the Arts. One may not be able to escape the thought that he saw his house and collection also as a monument to himself, and the placing of his own bust in the centre of the Museum justifies this claim.

We now come to the complicated part of the house. It is complex on two counts: one is the sequence of development of that part of the building which became the museum and the other, the continuous changes that are evident on the many plans that exist. The, at times, confusing series of plans begin in

June 1808 with Soane's intention of an addition eastwards of his office at the rear of No. 12. The former office became a library and was joined by a top-lit two-storey space shown on sketches as a »Plaister Room« and further east a two-storey »Upper« and »Lower Office«. All further schemes for the »Plaister Room« contain a fundamental idea: the penetration of daylight through two floors.

The first scheme, dated 13 June 1808, shows an upper level with a square opening in the ceiling and a floor slab independent from the north and south walls. In addition to these two slits, a long central opening, with rounded ends, made the floor a kind of bridge that allowed light and sight to the lower level. On this drawing the word »Museum« appears, and the lower level is defined as the »Crypt«. This is the first reference to this area as a museum and the basement as a crypt. Both are the seeds of an intention that was to dominate all subsequent designs. The museum idea is already evident as the enclosing walls show early arrangements of architectural fragments. The lower level shows a collection of funerary objects standing in wall recesses, a clear reference to ancient burial places that were excavated in Italy and most likely seen by Soane during his travels. Two low arched recesses in the walls increase the feeling of a sub-terranean crypt, a device that will dominate the future lower floor in the final design.

Two later sheets, of 8 and 29 July, bring us nearer to the eventual structure of the dome that is today's central feature of the Museum. The earlier design is the first idea of a domed space in the form of a sail-vault with four semi-circular fanlights. The second variant is a vault formed of solid pendentives and a glazed dome. Finally, with a section drawn by his pupil George Bailey, we arrive at the existing configuration of the »Dome« as it is now known. This drawing dates from May 1810 and supersedes the earlier attempts at a visual connection of the two levels. There a central opening, with narrow passages on two sides, permits a clear view of the crypt, with more daylight penetrating the darkening recesses below their arches. This may have been a design by Bailey himself, as it was exhibited in his name. The drawing also shows two small insets, one of which is a plan which reveals an early idea that may have been contemplated by Soane. It is a scheme whereby the ground floor of No. 13 is shown as an L-shaped gallery around a rectangular courtyard opening into the part of today's Museum gallery. Clearly this floor was envisaged entirely as a museum area, accessible from the entrance hall of No. 12. The significance of this proposal is the pervading idea that his residence should be the inspiration of which he so persistently dreamed. His statement in his *Description* of 1835 is exemplified in this plan: »The union and close connection between Painting, Sculpture and Architecture, Music and Poetry«, with his collection »as studies for my own mind and being intended similarly to benefit the Artist of future generations.«

With the ground behind No. 14 available for completing the sequence of rooms, Soane designed his picture-gallery that must, by any measure, be considered a brilliant solution. In an area the size of a small living-room (approximately 4 by 3.7 metres) he invented double layers of walls on three sides, enabling him to enlarge the display surface for pictures three times the length of the room. Full height hinged panels, above cabinets, open out and reveal an inner layer. The two complete series of paintings by William Hogarth (»A Rake's Progress« and »An Election«) are not only equalled, but, to the student of Architecture, surpassed by an accumulation of the master's work, together with Piranesi's Paestum drawings and paintings by Watteau and Turner, several drawings by Clerisseau and, above all, by the stunning water-colours by Gandy, his brilliant assistant. The greatest of them is a fantasy of more than one hundred of Soane's buildings, shown either as models, or in drawings set in a chamber crowned by the Soanean hallmark – the pendentive and shallow dome.

Opening both layers of the south wall a view unfolds that, even after the many surprises within the house, ranks as the epitome of Soane's spatial inventiveness. This is truly a »deus ex machina«. »Beautiful and attractive as the pictures certainly are, yet will the eye of the spectator frequently stray from them to that open portion of the room in which we can look down upon the Monk's Parlour, and where, in a beautiful recess, lighted through the medium of richly coloured glass stands the Nymph of Westmacott.«[8] This restrained description does not adequately describe the multiple effect of a device that, in its section, might well have been conceived some hundred years later with the multiple level inventions of Le Corbusier.

By limiting the south wall of the Picture-Room by just 1 metre inside the line of the main transverse wall of the museum, and by extending a rectangular bay in the centre into the courtyard, Soane created a vertical volume that extends to the lowest level. A skylight crowns this bay and diffuses a further theatrical effect on the statue of the nymph and the crowded retreat of the monk below. This is pure three-dimensional thinking that had to await the structural freedom of later times.

Before descending into the darker world of the Crypt, the Picture-Room and the complex sequence of spaces of the museum and Upper Drawing-Office must be described. The Picture-Room, already referred to, is a daringly vertical volume of almost 7 metres in height. Its ceiling could be defined as a Jacobean fantasy of richly decorated stalactites, as a canopy reaching downwards, that floats over clerestory lights on three sides.

The narrow Corridor in front of the Picture-Room is a claustrophobic space of casts of which, on the end wall, the huge capital and cornice from the Temple of Castor and Pollux in Rome almost burst the confines of the walls. At the other end a winding stair connects to the Upper Drawing-Office, supported by a colonnade of ten Corinthian columns. Here again the master of small spaces and multi-level connections limits the office floor to the width of the columnar supports and allows, by means of apertures to the north and south, light to fall from long skylights above onto the side walls, illuminating the many antique fragments that hang on them.

Above, a platform in space, so daringly independent of the main structure, shows the mastery of three-dimensional thinking. The Drawing-Office, so close to the source of daylight, makes for perfect conditions for drafting. The ever-present multifarious architectural casts exert the presence he strove to instil in his assistants in an ambience he describes as »peculiarly

16. Dome area, No. 13 Lincoln's Inn Fields, entitled »View of various architectural subjects belonging to John Soane Esq. R. A. as arranged in May MDCCX«. George Bailey. (SJSM, Drawer 14/6/3)

17. Picture-Room, No. 13 Lincoln's Inn Fields. (John Soane, *Description of the House and Museum*, London 1832, plate 10)

18. Joseph Michael Gandy, »Public and private buildings, executed by Sir John Soane between 1780 & 1815.«, 1818. (SJSM, P 87)

adapted for study«. The cunningly placed opening at the west end, giving a bird's-eye view of the Dome area, must have been a visual proof, for those working up there, of their master's gift for creating a continuum of spaces. Today these spatial interconnections are part of our architectural language, but in 1821 these effects were visionary.

Below, cupboards between the columns once housed some of the 54 volumes of drawings by the Adam brothers – just one of many valuable collections that Soane acquired. The low, cramped passage, densely filled with statues and fragments, is a characteristic device making the entry into the brightly lit Dome area so effective.

On four piers sits the one large skylight that, in contrast to the many other light-sources, is fully revealed and, apart from the courtyards, gives the one clear sight of the open sky. This clear illumination from above works its full effect on the spatial drama that unfolds as one approaches the balustrades that protect the square void to the Crypt. On the west side stands the famous statue of the Apollo Belvedere with his voluminous drapery over neck and outstretched left arm. Facing him, on the opposite rail, is the marble bust of the creator of this stage set, sculpted by his friend Sir Francis Chantrey and presented to him in 1830. (Chantrey said in a letter: »Will you come to me on Thursday morning and bring your Head with you?«)[9] Surrounding these centre-pieces are large collections of cinerary vases, panels from sarcophagi, a

bust of a Roman lady and fragmentary casts on the piers and flanking walls that ascend towards the pendentives, where the expected solid of the hemisphere of a dome is displaced by glass. Busts and frieze fragments crowd upwards and only the glazed dome seems to limit their ascent. Prior to 1890 the view towards the west ended with a recess lined with bookcases, but beyond this former recess is the New Picture Room, built in 1889/90 to the design of the then Curator, James Wild. It occupies the space of Soane's first drawing-office behind No. 12 – where all this began.

The walk through the upper parts of the house and Museum is now completed, and a descent into the twilight of the Crypt tempts. This temptation comes from the sight of a sarcophagus in the centre of the void below the Dome. This open coffin was Soane's most treasured prize, the alabaster resting place of Pharaoh Seti I, found in the Seti burial chamber in the Valley of the Kings at Thebes by the famous egyptologist Giovanni Battista Belzoni in 1817. The insatiable Soane purchased it in 1824, after the British Museum declined to buy it for £ 2,000. The pride of the ageing collector was appropriate, and a year later Soane gave candle-lit parties on three evenings. When candles were placed inside the sarcophagus this thin-walled limestone »flesh-eater« must have glowed in golden colours, revealing the exquisite hieroglyphs and scenes showing the deeds of the monarch. The bottom is engraved with the figure of the sky-goddess

19

UNION OF ARCHITECTURE, SCULPTURE, & PAINTING.

PL. XIII

Drawn & Engraved by H. Shaw.

19. Monk's Parlour, No. 13 Lincoln's Inn Fields. H. Shaw. (John Britton, *The Union of Architecture, Sculpture and Painting*, London, 1827, plate 13)
20. Sepulchral Chamber with the Sarcophagus of Seti I, No. 13 Lincoln's Inn Fields. B. Winkles after G. Moore. (John Britton, *The Union of Architecture, Sculpture and Painting*, London, 1827, plate 7)
21. Daniel Maclise (?), John Soane in old age. (SJSM, Drawer 69/3/6)

John Soane (signature)

Nut, a wholly appropriate deity, as she is always represented arcing over the land, her naked elongated body spanning the skies. To the creator of beautiful ceilings she is a true symbol.

The Sepulchral Chamber branches out, past circular headed arches into a sequence of »catacombs« of diminishing light. The extensive cellar, lit only by windows at the bottom of the two courtyards, symbolises the architect's morbid fascination with death.

Belonging to this sunken region is the last of the surprises – the »Parloir of Padre Giovanni«: the choice of the name is only too obvious and its »gothick« stage setting should hardly be taken too seriously. This Monk's Parlour, created at the same time as the Picture Room of 1824, is a glimpse into the dark romantic side of Soane's personality. This medieval influence, increased by his introverted, melancholy character, more apparent after the vindictive behaviour of his younger son, may well be the explanation for this dim and joyless retreat. But even here he played with the colours of stained glass and mirror reflections. He tended to brood here in his last years, leaving clarity and light above him. Did he ever, one wonders, look up, with the picture panels hinged open, and enjoy the space so full of surprises he created and take comfort in the tempting body of Westmacott's nymph?

He certainly looked out into the morbid Monk's Yard, with the grave of his wife's beloved dog Fanny, and the decaying gothic arcade taken from the old Palace of Westminster, turned into a fictitious ruin. In a strange unpublished text of 1812, entitled »Crude Hints towards the history of my house in Lincoln's Inn Fields«, Soane fantasises that his house was in ruins. A traveller of the future, coming across these Piranesian remains, speculates on what he may have found, ruminating that »the principal front was probably next the great square and as far as may be judged from the present state it must have been raised by some fanciful mind smitten with the love of novelty in direct defiance of all established rules of the architectural schools«. Love of »novelty«, in defiance of prevailing architectural rules, was Soane's legacy in the creation of this house and, thanks to the Act of Parliament of 1833, No. 13 Lincoln's Inn Fields is not a romantic ruin, like so many of his works, but a living monument to one of the greatest English architects. It is also living proof that the understanding of the beauties of the past shall inspire Soanean spirits to lead us into the future.

No. 13 is the house of an exceptional talent and vision. The great number of documents, so carefully preserved, offer an unusually full picture of Soane as a man of remarkable energy, of true professionalism, of honest work and of passion, even generosity. He directed his life towards a single goal – the creation of beauty that for him, and for us, who can admire his work, makes for pleasure and well-being.

Not surprisingly reality was more complex. The man Soane, despite all efforts, suffered hurtful setbacks of which his sons' defections were probably the hardest; and it may not be wrong to assume that his beloved wife's death was hastened by these pains. Soane lived with his personal grief, but it never limited his creative urge. The Aladdin's cave that he made and lived in for 23 years, 20 of which as a widower, was, amongst his very great number of buildings, the richest of them all. There he worked incessantly, but also enjoyed the company of friends, and both must have helped him to surmount his innermost difficulties.

Much could be gleaned to describe this complex man, but it may suffice to end this review of his house and museum by a revealing sketch, drawn towards the end of his life and from a personal observation of his final years.

George Wightwick, a young man who became Soane's secretary in his last years, offers, with his keen eyes and understanding of his employer's character, an authentic picture of John Soane the man: »… It is true, he was ill when I saw him, and sorely worn with perplexity and vexation; and therefore I ought to say, that at that time, it can be scarcely said that he had any front face. In profile his countenance was extensive … A brown wig carried the elevation of his head to the utmost attainable height; so that, altogether, his physiognomy was suggestive of the picture which is presented on the back of a spoon held vertically. His eyes now sadly failing in their sight, looked red and small beneath their full lids; but, through their weakened orbs, the fire of his spirit would often show itself, in proof of its unimpaired vigour. Finally, his countenance presented, under different circumstances, two distinct phases … a delicate sensibility spiced with humour; towards men, a politeness in which condescension and respect were mingled; and towards women, a suavity, enlivened with a show of gallantry, rather sly than shy. The other phase … indicated an acute sensitiveness, and a fearful irritability, dangerous to himself, if not to others: an embittered heart, prompting a cutting and sarcastic mind; a contemptuous disregard for the feeling of his dependants; and yet, himself, the very victim of irrational impulses; with no pity for the trials of his neighbour, and nothing but frantic despair under his own …«[10]

As so often, great creators of beauty and harmony remain vulnerable and open to suffering. This is often disguised by powerful assertiveness as a defence. John Soane was no exception.

It seems most appropriate to end this account of Soane's life and of his most personal work by recalling the words of the Roman poet Sallust crowning a remarkable façade by Piranesi, Soane's guiding spirit: »novitatem meam contemnunt ego illorum ignaviam« (they despise my novelty, I their timidity).

Notes

[1] Dorothy Stroud, *Sir John Soane, Architect*, London, 1984, pp. 23, 24.

[2] Dorothy Stroud, op. cit., p. 24.

[3] Dorothy Stroud, op. cit., p. 57.

[4] Dorothy Stroud, op. cit., p. 65.

[5] *A new Description of Sir John Soane's Museum*, 7th revised edition, London, 1986, p. 31.

[6] John Summerson, »Sir John Soane and the Furniture of Death«, *The Unromantic Castle & Other Essays*, London, 1990, p. 135.

[7] Arthur T. Bolton, *The Works of Sir John Soane*, London, 1924, p. XVII.

[8] *Popular Description of Sir John Soane's House, Museum & Library*, written in 1835 by Mrs. Barbara Hofland, edited by Arthur T. Bolton, Oxford, 1919, p. 21.

[9] Arthur T. Bolton, *The Portrait of Sir John Soane*, London, 1927, p. 453.

[10] Arthur T. Bolton, op. cit., p. 400.

5. The Library looking south.
6. Detail of the Library showing the arches above the
bookcases and one of the projecting piers dividing the
Library from the Dining-Room.

7. The Dining-Room looking north into the Monument Court.
8. Detail of the Dining-Room with the portrait of Sir John Soane by Sir Thomas Lawrence.

10. The Dressing-Room and the Study looking south into the Dining-Room.

11. The lantern of the Dressing-Room, the upper part of which is a model of the dome of the Freemasons' Hall, London, built by Sir John Soane in 1828–30.

12. The Dressing-Room Lobby looking south into the Dressing-Room and the Study with bust of Palladio.

15. Detail of the spherical
ceiling in the Breakfast
Parlour.

16. One of the convex mirrors in the sprandrels of the ceiling in the Breakfast Parlour.

17. The South Drawing-Room looking south.
18. The Loggia in the South Drawing-Room looking west.

21. The Colonnade looking west.
22. Detail showing the back of the bust of Sir John Soane by Sir Francis Leggatt Chantrey, the Apollo Belvedere in the Dome area and the portrait of Sir John Soane by Christopher William Hunneman in the New Picture-Room.

p. 44/45
23. The Dome area looking east.

24. The Dome area looking east with the opening to the Upper Drawing-Office behind the bust of Sir Thomas Lawrence by R.W. Sievier.

27. Detail of the Dome area showing the busts of Sir John Soane by Sir Francis Leggatt Chantrey and of Sir Thomas Lawrence by R. W. Sievier.

28. The Upper Drawing-Office with the opening to the
Dome.
29. Detail of the Upper Drawing-Office.

31. Detail of the Corridor showing the terracotta relief »Britannia attended by Peace and Plenty« by John Bacon the Elder.

33. The Picture-Room looking east with planes opened.

34. Detail of the Picture-Room with the south planes opened to show the Nymph by Sir Richard Westmacott in the Picture-Room Recess.

36. The Monk's Parlour looking west towards the Crypt.
37. The Crypt looking east towards the Monk's Parlour.

38. The Crypt looking west towards the Sarcophagus of Seti I.

39. A stone canopy from the east front of St Stephen's Chapel, Westminster, in the Crypt.

40. The Monument Court
seen from the Crypt.

Chronology

1753 John Soan born on 10 September in Goring, Berkshire.
1768 Came to London and entered George Dance's office.
1770 About this year entered the office of Henry Holland.
1772 Won Royal Academy Silver Medal for measured drawing of the Banqueting House.
1776 Won Royal Academy Gold Medal for a design for a Triumphal Bridge.
1778 Left for Italy on 18 March.
1780 Returned from Italy.
1784 Married Elizabeth Smith, niece of George Wyatt, a wealthy builder. Began to spell his name Soane.
1786 John Soane junior born.
1788 Appointed architect to the Bank of England.
1789 George Soane born.
1792 No. 12 Lincoln's Inn Fields built for his own occupation. Moved in in 1794.
1795 Associate of the Royal Academy.
1800 Acquired Pitzhanger Manor, Ealing. Rebuilt it until 1804 as a country retreat.
1802 Royal Academician.
1806 Appointed Professor of Architecture at the Royal Academy.
1808 Bought No. 13 Lincoln's Inn Fields.
1809 Started his Academy Lectures.
1812 No. 13 Lincoln's Inn Fields rebuilt.
1815 Mrs Soane died on 22 November.
1823 Eldest son, John, died on 21 October.
1824 Rebuilt No. 14 Lincoln's Inn Fields.
1833 Retired as Architect to the Bank of England. The Act of Parliament »for the settling and preserving« the Museum received the Royal Assent.
1835 Was presented a Gold Medal by the Architects of England.
1837 Sir John Soane died on 20 January.

Selected bibliography

John Britton, *The Union of Architecture, Sculpture and Painting*, London, 1827.
Arthur T. Bolton, *The Works of Sir John Soane*, London, 1924.
Arthur T. Bolton (ed.), *Lectures on Architecture by Sir John Soane,* London, 1925.
Arthur T. Bolton, *The Portrait of Sir John Soane*, London, 1927.
John Summerson, *Sir John Soane*, London, 1952.
Dorothy Stroud, *The Architecture of Sir John Soane*, London, 1961.
P. de la Ruffinière du Prey, *John Soane: The Making of an Architect*, London, 1982.
John Summerson, David Watkin and G.-Tilman Mellinghoff, *John Soane*, London and New York, 1983.
Dorothy Stroud, *Sir John Soane, Architect*, London, 1984.
Susan Feinberg Millenson, *Sir John Soane's Museum*, Ann Arbor, Mich., 1987.